D0833110

Kids' Questions
about
God and Jesus

Kids' Questions about God and Jesus

Cheryl Fawcett
Robert C. Newman

Illustrations by Ron Mazellan

Regular Baptist Press
1300 North Meacham Road
Schaumburg, Illinois 60173

*To my nieces and nephews, all of
whom are following Jesus: Melissa,
Monica, Amanda, Erin, Matthew,
Carrie, Andrew, Ben, and Madelyn
I love you!*—Aunt Cheryl

*To Barbara and Brian, Charles
and Pat, Donna and Daniel,
Roberta and Doug.
Your dad and friend, gone on before,
eagerly awaiting your arrival in
Heaven.*—Robert C. Newman

Scripture quotations marked NKJV are from the New King James Version of the Bible. Copyright © 1979, 1980, 1982 by Thomas Nelson, Inc. Used by permission. All rights reserved. All other quotations are from the King James Version.

KIDS' QUESTIONS ABOUT GOD AND JESUS

© 2003, 1994 (formerly published as part of *I Have a Question about God*)

Regular Baptist Press • Schaumburg, Illinois

1-800-727-4400 • www.regularbaptistpress.org

Printed in U.S.A.

All rights reserved

RBP5304 • ISBN: 1-59402-081-7

Contents

Preface

Ten years ago the book *I Have a Question about God* was published. In the years since then, we have received many letters and face-to-face stories of how God has used its contents to bring children to faith. Others have shared that children have decided to be baptized. Many adults have shared that the truth simply told and wrapped in a modern story has made theology come alive for them. Many have reported steps of growth in the lives of both parent and child.

My coauthor, Robert Newman, is with the Lord now. His impact on my life and ministry left an indelible mark I never want to get over. The strong desire that he and I shared to provide a tool for parents to teach their children some first steps with God has not diminished or changed. If anything, my resolve has grown stronger.

Kids' Questions about God

Hints and Helps

Keep it simple! Take, for example, Genesis1:1: "In the beginning God created the heaven and the earth." This statement is profound yet simple. To the scientist and the young child alike, the Bible says one thing. God is before all that we know and see, and He made all that we know and see. The Scriptures do not debate God; they affirm Him without question. He is! He does! Most important is for us to call children to faith, not provide them with a detailed explanation.

Verse to Memorize

Jonah 4:2: "I know that you are a gracious and merciful God, slow to anger, and abundant in lovingkindness, one who relents from doing harm" (NKJV).

Who Is God?

H i! My name is Topher. Really my name is Christopher, but my friends call me Toph or Topher. I'm eight. I like to ride my bike and play T-ball, soccer, and basketball. I have two sisters, Megan and Bobbie. Megan is ten and plays the piano all the time. She takes lessons. Roberta is four. We call her Bobbie. She's fun to tease, but she drives me nuts, always asking, "What's that?" or "What does this mean?" Mom and Dad say she'll grow out of always asking questions, but I doubt it.

She did it just yesterday. In the afternoon a man came to our house. Bobbie ran to the door, and right after Mom opened it, she asked, "Who are you?"

"Bobbie," Mom said.

But the man smiled. "I'm a firefighter. I help people when they are sick and need to get to the hospital or when they have a crash in their car or when their house catches on fire. Right now I'm collecting money for the fire department."

The firefighter talked to Mom for a while. I think she even gave him some money. When he left, Bobbie asked right away, "What is a fireman like?"

"He told you he helps people, Bobbie." I had to remind her.

"But what is he like?" Bobbie asked the same question again.

Mom answered that time. "He is helpful and hardworking. He is a fine neighbor."

"Is God like that too? Would He be a good neighbor?"

Mom was quiet for a minute. I could tell she was thinking. "No one has ever asked me that before, Bobbie," she finally said. "I'm not sure how to answer you. When I was a little girl, I went to church and read the Bible a lot, but it's been a long time. Let me think . . . God is holy."

"What does 'holy' mean?" When Mom answers one question, Bobbie always asks another one. See why I go crazy?

She told Bobbie, "'Holy' means that God is set apart from sin. We can think of sin as being dirty and holy as being clean. I remember, too, that angels called out that God is holy, holy, holy."[1]

"That means God is really, really, really clean. Does He take a lot of baths?"

"No, it means He does what is right."

"How does He know what is right?"

"He is God, and whatever He does is right. He knows everything too, so He knows everything that is right and wrong."

I asked Mom, "You mean God never does anything wrong?"

"No, never."

Bobbie said, "I wish I was God so I would never do anything wrong."

I laughed. "Bobbie, you can't be God."

Mom told us, "You both can be like Him. He wants you to do what is right all the time."

"Does God love me?"

"Yes, He does, Bobbie."

"Does He love Toph?"

"God loves everyone!"

"Even Michael Lobatosky?"

"Yes, even Michael."

"Does He love Mikki, our cat?"

"Yes, God loves all the creatures. He made them, you know."

"I think God would be a good neighbor."

"Yes, Bobbie, I think He would be the best neighbor you could ever have."

Verses to Read

John 3:16: "For God so loved the world that He gave His only begotten

Son, that whoever believes in Him should not perish but have everlasting life" (NKJV).

Leviticus 11:44: "For I am the Lord your God. You shall therefore sanctify yourselves, and you shall be holy; for I am holy" (NKJV).

Genesis 1:1: "In the beginning God created the heaven and the earth."

1. Isaiah 6:1–3

QUESTIONS TO ASK YOUR CHILD

✳

1. *What is God like?*

2. *What does "holy" mean?*

3. *How can you be holy?*

Where Does God Live?

On the first day of school, Megan was dressed and ready early. She always is. Mom had to help Bobbie put on the new clothes we had bought the week before at some big department store. I was supposed to be brushing my teeth, but I got to playing with some toys in the bathroom sink.

Then Mom called, "Hurry now, everyone, or you'll be late!" She gave each of us a kiss at the front door. We practically ran to the corner and waited for the school bus. When it came, we jumped on and found seats. Megan and Bobbie sat right behind the bus driver; I sat behind them with my friend Tommy.

Megan started asking Bobbie questions about her address and phone number. See, it was Bobbie's first day at preschool, and she needed to know that stuff. "Where do you live, Bobbie?" Megan asked.

"In that big blue house."

"No, I mean what is your house number and street name?"

"Ummm . . . 1022 Brewster Courthouse."

"It's just Court, Bobbie, not courthouse," I told her. "The court-house is downtown."

"Oh yeah, you're right."

"What's your town?" Megan continued.

"It's the one after we go through the big bridge over the river."

"What is its name, silly?" I think Megan was getting a little impatient.

"It's Grafton. Mom told you not to call me silly," Bobbie told her. Then Bobbie looked out the window and was actually quiet for a few seconds before she asked, "Megan, where does God live?"

"I don't know. Let's ask the bus driver." We were at a stoplight, so Megan tapped the bus driver on the shoulder. He's a nice man. He's driven my school bus two years. "Mr. Bus Driver, where does God live?" Megan asked him. I couldn't hear his answer. When Megan sat back down, I asked her what he had said.

"He doesn't know either. He said we should ask our mom and dad."

Bobbie had a good first day at school. She remembered our house number and street name and even the name of our town without any help. And she remembered her question too. When Mom picked her up from preschool, the first thing she said was, "Where does God live?"

Mom told her, "He lives very far away."

"You mean like by Grandma and Grandpa? They live really, really far away."

"Farther than that," Mom tried to explain. "He lives out of this world."

"Like Star Wars!"

"No, Bobbie, Star Wars is pretend. God lives in a real place. He lives in a place the Bible calls Heaven."

"Is it a pretend, make-believe place?" I think Bobbie was confused. Actually, I was kind of confused too.

Mom found her Bible and looked in the back part under the word "Heaven." She found a place and read to us. "'For God is in heaven, and thou upon earth: therefore let thy words be few.' Ecclesiastes 5:2. There it is. God is in Heaven, and you are on earth. It reminds me of a song I learned when I was your age. 'Heaven is a wonderful place. Filled with glory and grace. I want to see my Savior's face. Heaven is a wonderful, Heaven is a glorious, Heaven is a wonderful place.'"

Verse to Read

Acts 17:24: "God, who made the world and everything in it, since He is Lord of heaven and earth, does not dwell in temples made with hands" (NKJV).

QUESTIONS TO ASK YOUR CHILD

1. Where does the Bible say God lives?

2. Can you see Heaven? Why not?

3. Since Heaven is so far away, how can you know God lives there?

Does God Have a Wife?

My dad's great! He's a carpenter, so he works with wood and nails and ladders and saws and stuff like that. Sometimes he takes me to see the houses he builds. That's the greatest!

One time last summer, Mom and Megan were going to Eastman to buy a new book for piano lessons. I don't like shopping very much, so I asked to go with Dad. Of course, when Bobbie heard me ask, she wanted to go too.

When we got to the place, I saw a big woodpile and a huge hole in the ground. Dad's workers had put concrete into the ground to make "footers." I think that's what Dad said.

We met Dad's helpers, John and Kirby. I saw Kirby lift six boards by himself! Bobbie and I moved one board a little ways. Then Dad told us to play on a pile of sand while he, John, and Kirby put in the floorboards or something.

Bobbie's not bad—for a girl. She likes to play with trucks, and she doesn't care if she gets dirty. I had three trucks, and we made lots of roads in the sand. We had fun until lunch.

I had taken only one bite of my sandwich when Bobbie started asking crazy questions again. "John, do you have a mother?"

"She meant, 'Do you have a wife?' I think." I had to help since Bobbie doesn't always say the right words.

"Yeah, do you have a wife?" Bobbie asked.

"I sure do." John was smiling. "She's beautiful and kind, and she loves me a lot."

Then Bobbie asked, "Kirby, do you have a mother? I mean wife?" Kirby didn't say anything. He just looked . . . kind of red. Bobbie must have asked the wrong question again.

"He's working on it," John said, "but the girl doesn't know it yet. Actually, she does act more like his mother sometimes. That's probably why he's turning all red."

"I am not red! But I do have a great girlfriend. I like her a lot. We're getting to know each other better. I hope someday she'll be my wife."

Then Kirby smiled funny at my dad and asked him, "Gary, how about you? Do you have a wife, or 'mother,' as Bobbie likes to say?" I thought that was the silliest question.

But Dad smiled and said, "I do indeed. She's the best woman I've ever known. I don't know what I'd do without her."

"Dad, does God have a wife?"

Bobbie said the right word, but what a question! "I mean, what would God do without a wife like Mom?"

"Well, actually, God is perfect in Himself."

Then Bobbie wanted to know, "What does 'perfect' mean?"

"It means God doesn't need anyone or anything to make Him better. He doesn't need anyone to help Him."

Dad stopped. I think he was thinking. Then he said, "The Bible does call God a father.[1] When we think of God in that way, we earth people can understand a little better what He is like."

"But will God ever find a wife?" Bobbie looked kind of worried.

"Actually, Muffin,"—I don't know why Dad calls her that—"God doesn't need to find a wife. There's no one on earth or in Heaven who is like Him. He is satisfied just like He is."

"God will get lonely without a wife."

Dad smiled again. "No, He won't. He knows that people get lonely though—just like Adam did. God made a helper who was perfect for Adam. She helped keep him company and was the mother of his children.

God allows us to have mothers and fathers and be children in families, but God does not have a wife."

"God has a Son."

"You're right, Bobbie. And we'll talk about that more when we get home tonight. Now you build roads with Toph while I finish this house floor."

"Okay." Bobbie grabbed the little red truck before she asked me, "Toph, did you know God doesn't need a wife?"

Verse to Read

Acts 17:25: "Nor is He [God] worshiped with men's hands, as though He needed anything, since He gives to all life, breath, and all things" (NKJV).

1. 1 Corinthians 8:6

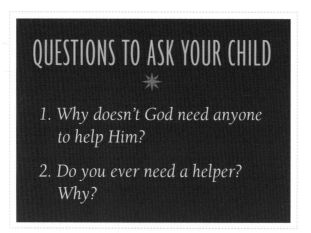

QUESTIONS TO ASK YOUR CHILD

1. *Why doesn't God need anyone to help Him?*

2. *Do you ever need a helper? Why?*

Does God Have Any Children?

I guess Megan and Mom had a good trip to Eastman. They found the music book they wanted, and Megan said she tried out new pianos. I'm glad I wasn't there. Megan also said they ate lunch at Burger World. Mom brought Bobbie and me the meal box toys. They were these little plastic people things.

Bobbie put her toy girl on the table at dinnertime. "Toph, where's your little boy?"

"I left him in my room." I was thinking about something else. "Mom, you know that new Carter family down the street? How many kids do they have?"

"They have four children."

"That's what I thought, but yesterday I saw six kids playing in the backyard. They told me they all live there."

"Oh, the Carters have two foster children." Dad passed me the hamburger hot dish.

"What are foster children?"

"They're children who have had trouble in their own family and need a place to stay for a while."

"But are Mr. and Mrs. Carter their mom and dad?"

"Well, the Carters are act-ing as their mom and dad."

"Forever?"

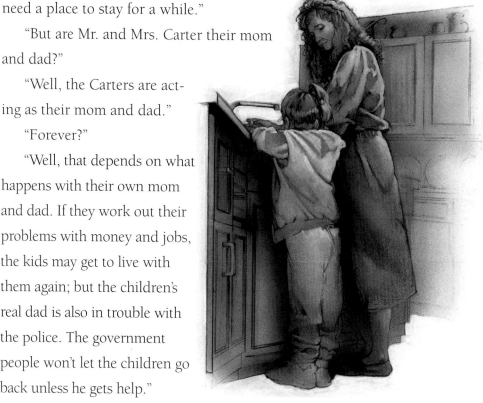

"Well, that depends on what happens with their own mom and dad. If they work out their problems with money and jobs, the kids may get to live with them again; but the children's real dad is also in trouble with the police. The government people won't let the children go back unless he gets help."

"What if their dad doesn't get help? Who will be their family then?" Dad said the Carters might adopt the kids if their parents didn't get help.

"What does 'adopt' mean?" Bobbie asked that.

"It means to choose children to be part of your family."

"Mom, does God have a son?"

"The Bible calls Jesus God's Son, but it's not exactly like human fathers and sons. Have you heard John 3:16? 'For God so loved the world, that he gave his only begotten Son, that whosoever believeth in him should not perish, but have everlasting life.'" Of course, Megan said she knew that whole thing.

"Mom, does God have any girls?"

"No, He has only one Son, Jesus," Mom said.

"Maybe God could adopt a girl. Maybe He could adopt lots of girls."

22

Mom had her Bible open, and I could tell she was going to read something.

"Here's the verse. John 1:12. It does talk about people becoming God's children—boys and girls. 'But as many as received Him, to them He gave the right to become children of God' (NKJV). God is a father to people who trust Jesus as Savior."

"Forever?" Bobbie asked.

"Yes, forever. Just like the Carters, God will keep loving His adopted children. He may correct us, but we will always be His children once we believe on Him."

"Mom, did God adopt you?"

"Yes, Bobbie, when I was a little girl. I would like you to think about being adopted into God's family too."

Verse to Memorize

John 1:12: "But as many as received Him, to them He gave the right to become children of God, to those who believe in His name" (NKJV).

QUESTIONS TO ASK YOUR CHILD

1. Who is God's Son?

2. How can you be adopted into God's family?

3. Once you have been adopted into God's family, how long will you belong to His family?

How Old Is God?

The Schmidts' neighbor Mrs. Greene is really old. She needs lots of help, so Mom is always taking Bobbie and Megan to see her and do stuff for her.

Mrs. Greene lives in a really old house. The sidewalk is all broken and crooked. The shutters on the windows are about to fall off. The mailbox is rusted. Weeds are everywhere. Mom said that Mrs. Greene's house used to be the prettiest one on the street.

Since Mrs. Greene can't walk too well anymore, she uses a walker to help her move without falling. Whenever Bobbie rings the doorbell, it takes Mrs. Greene a long time to answer the door.

Bobbie usually finds some flowers and takes them to Mrs. Greene to cheer her up.

Not too long ago, it was Mrs. Greene's birthday. Bobbie took flowers as usual, and Megan had helped Mom bake a small cake and decorate it. They took that too.

Bobbie rang the doorbell. Mrs. Greene's doorbell makes a really

loud DING DONG! While they waited, Bobbie, Megan, and Mom decided to sing to Mrs. Greene when she got to the door.

"Happy birthday to you! Happy birthday to you! Happy birthday, Mrs. Greene! Happy birthday to you!"

"How old are you anyway?" Bobbie and her questions did it again!

"It's not polite to ask a lady her age, Bobbie." Mom said that quickly before Mrs. Greene could catch her breath and answer.

"Are you 200?" Bobbie doesn't know when to stop asking questions.

"Bobbie, please apologize to Mrs. Greene," Mom told her.

"I'm sorry." Bobbie looked at her shoes. She does that when she feels bad.

"That's okay, honey. I'm old but not that old yet. Actually this is my eighty-third birthday. I just feel like 200 some days."

Mrs. Greene liked her cake and flowers. Mom, Bobbie, and Megan had a little party with her. Then on the way home, Bobbie started asking questions again. "Mom, how old are you?"

"As old as my tongue and a little older than my teeth," answered Mom.

"How old is Dad?"

"Oh, much older than I am," Mom said. Mom was teasing. At least, she was smiling.

"How old is Mikki, our cat?"

"In people years she's about 60."

"How old is God?"

"Too old to count."

"Why?"

Mom answered her. "Well, the Bible says that before God made the world, He was there. The Bible uses the word 'eternal' to describe Him."

"What's 'eternal' mean?"

"It means without beginning or ending. God never had a birthday."

"You mean He never gets a birthday cake? How does He remember how old He is? Is God too old to walk, like Mrs. Greene?"

"God is different from people. We are born. We count our years one at a time, and we die. God always was and always will be. We can't count His years because they never started and will never end. God doesn't have a body like you and me do. He is perfect. He never gets old or worn out."

Then Megan said, "It's like God is forever young and never old."

"Something like that, honey."

Verses to Read

Deuteronomy 33:27: "The eternal God is your refuge, and underneath are the everlasting arms" (NKJV).

Psalm 90:2: "Before the mountains were brought forth, or ever You had formed the earth and the world, even from everlasting to everlasting, You are God" (NKJV).

QUESTIONS TO ASK YOUR CHILD

✳

1. Does God have a birthday? Why not?

2. What does "eternal" mean?

Does God Get Tired, Hungry, or Sleepy?

The night before we went to Grandma and Grandpa's house, I couldn't wait for morning! I kept looking at my alarm clock all night long, wishing it would say 6:00. We live in Ohio, and it takes us a long time to get to where they live.

All our suitcases were ready. We only had to put on our clothes, eat some cereal, and brush our teeth. Megan helped Dad with the suitcases.

Bobbie was getting some books to read on the way—well, actually for me to read to her. I helped Mom get finished up in the kitchen. We were ready to go.

All morning we just looked out the car windows. The corn was growing. And we saw lots of cows in the fields. We played the license plate game for a while. I won! We stopped at a rest area and ate a picnic lunch that Mom had packed. Bobbie ran around and rolled in the grass. When we got back in the car, Bobbie asked me to read to her. I read all ten books—two times each.

But Bobbie was still not happy. She kept wiggling. Mom says we're "restless" when we're like that. Then Bobbie began to cry. "Are we almost there? I'm tired. I'm hungry."

"Take a little nap, and we'll be there soon," Mom told her.

"I can't; there's no room back here. I'm tired, Mom. I'm hungry."

Mom had some snacks packed in the back, so Dad stopped at the next rest stop and got them out. Pretzels and apples helped a little. Mom got out a surprise book for Bobbie to color too.

Bobbie colored for a while, but we still had a long way to go before we would get to Grandpa and Grandma's.

"I'm tired! I'm hungry! Aren't we there yet?"

"No, not yet; but we are much closer, Bobbie."

Bobbie put her head on Megan's lap for a second. Then she sat up again. "Mom, does God ever get tired and hungry? Does God ever sleep?"

Mom had been reading her Bible to help pass the time, and I guess she was at a good place to answer Bobbie. "Listen as I read to you from Psalm 121. 'My help cometh from the LORD, which made heaven and earth . . . he that keepeth thee will not slumber. Behold, he that keepeth Israel—'"

"What's Israel?"

"Israel is a nation that God chose as His special people. God watches over them in extra special ways. 'He that keepeth Israel shall neither slumber nor sleep.'"

"What's 'slumber'?"

"'Slumber' is another way to say 'sleep.'"

"Would God sleep if He had to ride in the car a long time?"

"Well, Bobbie, God doesn't need to travel anywhere because He is everywhere at the same time."

I wish I could be everywhere. It must be great being God. He never gets tired or hungry, and He never has to sit in a crowded backseat.

Verses to Read

Psalm 121

QUESTIONS TO ASK YOUR CHILD

1. Does God ever sleep?

2. Why doesn't God have to travel from one place to another?

Does God Get Sick or Die?

Grandpa had just left for the sheep barn, and I asked Mom if I could go. Bobbie wanted to go too. There were new lambs, and we wanted to see them. Mom said we could, and we ran to catch up with Grandpa. The barn doesn't have any rooms—just these high feeder bins for the ewes. Ewes are girl sheep, and rams are boys. Grandpa had one really big ram tied up in a corner of the barn behind a fence. "Rams tend to be mean," Grandpa warned us.

That ram looked mean too. I wasn't going to go near him! When Grandpa fed the ram, it tried to hit him with its horns, and it knocked over the pail of grain Grandpa was going to feed it. Grandpa did let me throw some hay to the ram, but I didn't go inside its fence. When Grandpa came out, I moved out of the way!

When we got done in the barn, we went to check on some ewes that were out in the field with their baby lambs. Grandpa had me carry a pail of water to give the sheep. One ewe had one lamb, another ewe had twins, and another ewe had triplets. Grandpa said ewes don't usually have triplets. One of the triplet lambs was sick. I could tell which one it was right away because it was really small and lay very still. The other lambs were getting milk from their mothers, but the sick one couldn't even do that.

"Will that lamb die, Grandpa?" I wished Bobbie hadn't asked that.

"I don't know for sure, but in a few days we'll be able to tell better. I'll call the veterinarian this afternoon and ask her what I should do to help."

"I don't want the lamb to die, Grandpa. Is it very sick?"

"I think it'll probably be okay."

"Grandpa, does God get sick?"

Grandpa always tells us that he loves God, and he knows lots of stuff about God too. Grandpa can even answer Bobbie's really hard questions.

"That's a good question, Bobbie. Let's go back to the house, and I'll read to you from the Psalms. People and animals get sick. Sometimes our bodies don't work right. Sometimes we eat something that makes us sick. Sometimes we get sick from germs."

"I got the chicken pox from Toph."

"People get sick all the time," Grandpa said, "but God is a spirit. He is real, but He doesn't have a body like you and me. He doesn't get sick. He doesn't catch cold or get the flu or chicken pox. His heart never gets tired or worn out. He never breaks a bone because He has no bones."

"Why do we have to get sick then?" I wanted to know that. I had missed two T-ball games one time when I had the flu.

Grandpa started to answer. "When God made Adam, Adam was perfect. He would not get sick, and he would have lived forever. But Adam sinned. He disobeyed God. God had to punish Adam for eating the fruit God had told him to leave alone. The Bible says that Adam and everyone after him would die because he disobeyed."[1]

"That's a hard punishment!" I said.

I guess Bobbie was thinking the same thing. She asked, "Is God mean?"

"No, Bobbie, He's holy and just. He can't stand sin. But God did make a way for man to live forever with Him in Heaven through Jesus."

"My mom and dad tell me about Jesus," Bobbie said. "Does God ever die? Who would take care of the world and hold it together and make rain and sunshine?"

"Don't worry, Bobbie. God will never die. He will always be able to take care of people and animals and the earth. The Bible says, 'But You, O LORD, shall endure forever. . . . Your years are throughout all generations. . . . You laid the foundation of the earth. . . . They will

33

perish, but You will endure. . . . You are the same, and Your years will have no end'" (Psalm 102:12, 24–27; NKJV).

Verse to Read

Psalm 90:2: "Before the mountains were brought forth, or ever You had formed the earth and the world, even from everlasting to everlasting You are God" (NKJV).

1. Romans 5:18, 19

QUESTIONS TO ASK YOUR CHILD

✳

1. Will God ever get sick?

2. Will God ever die?

3. Why do you get sick?

How Do We Know about God?

We had to go to bed early, but that was okay. The next day we were going to the Hartford Fair! Grandpa told us about it at supper. "It's the granddaddy of all the fairs in our part of Pennsylvania. You can ride rides and see animals, beautiful flowers, crafts, and wood-working. The fair has lots of food and ice cream too!"

"Aunt Ginny and Uncle Bill always run the ice cream booth. They'll sell you a huge cone for only one dollar." Grandma smiled at me when she said that. She knows I like ice cream a lot. Megan got excited when Grandma told her about the music in the grandstand. Bobbie just wanted to see the sheep, goats, pigs, horses, and cows. We all wanted to go with Grandma to see if her pickles and corn would win any prizes.

The fair was great! It seemed like Grandpa knew everybody there. He took Megan and me into the craft display. We looked at lots of pic-tures with stitching.

"I think this one must have taken forever." Megan was pointing at the biggest picture in the row.

"Well, not forever, but a long time. The lady who made it is willing to work a long time on something to do good work."

"How do you know, Grandpa?" It was Bobbie! I hadn't even noticed that she was following us until she started her questions.

"Well, child, notice how even her stitches are. Every one is perfectly in line with the others. Look at the beautiful colors she chose. People show a lot about themselves in the things they make. You can tell which ladies are careful and take extra time. Look at this picture." He pointed to another picture.

"It's the same design." I said that.

"Who made that one, Grandpa? The colors are dull," Megan said.

"The tag on the frame says Mrs. Brown. I'm not surprised; she wears dull dresses too."

"Look at this blue ribbon, Grandpa!" I had gone down the row ahead of them. "Who d'ya think made this one?" I wanted Grandpa to guess.

"Why, that looks like your Grandma's work. I'd know it anywhere." Grandpa looked proud.

"You saw her doing it, didn't you, Grandpa?" Megan asked.

"No, I was outside with the sheep when she made this picture, but it is just like her. You can tell a person by his work, you know."

After we left the craft display, we rode rides and ate ice cream. Then we listened to music in the grandstands. Bobbie had to see all the animals and pet each one. I had so much fun I didn't want to leave, but the fair had to close down for the night.

Grandpa had to carry Bobbie to the car. I thought she was asleep until she asked, "Grandpa, how do you know so much about God? Did you see Him?"

"Well, not face-to-face, but I sure learn a lot by looking at all the beautiful things He made."

"What did God make, Grandpa?"

"See those beautiful hills over there? And the gorgeous stars? All those fruits and vegetables you saw today in the vegetable barn and at the 4-H display are God's work. The flowers we saw today are God's handiwork. And see those thunderclouds over there?"

"A big storm is coming. Is God mad?"

"No, Bobbie, He's just watering the earth so more of our crops will grow. I've traveled many places, and everywhere I go I learn more about how great and awesome my God really is."

"You learn about God from seeing the world?"

"Some of what I know, but not all. Do you remember today when we looked at the tags on the pictures?"

"The tags told about the ladies who made the pictures." Megan reminded Bobbie about them.

"Yes, I remember," Bobbie said. "Does the earth have a tag on it, Grandpa?" Bobbie's eyes were closed. She asks funnier questions when she's tired.

"Well, not actually a tag, but God gave us the Bible to tell us much more about Himself than we could ever have guessed by just looking at the things He made. Creation tells us some things, but the Bible helps us understand a lot more about God. Some people get so excited about what God made that they never take time to read more about Him."

Grandpa put Bobbie into the car, and she finally opened her eyes. "I will be able to read by myself pretty soon. Do you have a Bible for me?"

"I'm so glad you asked that, little one."

Verses to Read
Psalm 19

QUESTIONS TO ASK YOUR CHILD

1. What two things teach us about God?

2. By looking at what God has made, what do you think God is like?

Kids' Questions about Jesus

Hints and Helps

With this subject we reach an intricate and difficult problem. Orthodox Christianity has always believed in the doctrine of the Trinity, and we do too! But believing and explaining are sometimes extremely different tasks, especially when it comes to children. We will talk with you, the adult, about the Trinity. We will not endeavor to do the same with the children. But children can be good theologians, and they will ask you about the Trinity.

The Trinity is a tri-unity of persons. Historic Christianity teaches that God is one as manifested in three distinct Persons: "The LORD our God, the Lord is one!" (Deuteronomy 6:4; NKJV). Yet the Great Commission in Matthew 28:19 and 20 includes the baptismal formula that teaches God is the Father, the Son, and the Holy Spirit. Three Persons—yet one God! The structure of the language in Matthew strongly points out that each of these three Persons is equal.

Christianity is based on faith. Part of faith is believing in the Trinity simply because, according to the Scriptures, God is triune. We believe in a triune God because He declares Himself to be so, not because we fully comprehend the Trinity. If we could explain God, He wouldn't be God.

What's in a name? Everything! Parents often subtly predict the personality of their children when they choose their names. The name of

God's Son is the Lord Jesus Christ. He has other titles as well; each title is significant. "Lord" means "Master." "Jesus" is a Greek form of the Hebrew name "Joshua," which means "Jehovah is salvation." "Jehovah" is God's covenant, or relational, name to His special people Israel. "Christ" denotes Jesus' deity. It literally means "the anointed one."

By application of Jesus' names, we know that the Lord Jesus Christ desires to be three things in our lives. As Lord, Jesus desires to be the Master of your life. As Jesus, He longs to be your Savior from sin and punishment. As Christ, He is very God taking on the form of man. Therefore, He is familiar with all your limitations, sorrows, and sin without being touched or tainted by sin (Hebrews 4:14–16).

Verse to Memorize

Galatians 4:4: "But when the fulness at the time was come, God sent forth his Son, made of a woman, made under the law."

What Is Jesus Like?

Mom plays "Who Am I?" with us all the time. She describes a person, an animal, or a thing and asks, "Who am I?" Then we have to guess who or what it is.

One day when we were going to the library, Mom said, "Who am I? I have four legs. I like to eat grass. I give milk. I make a loud sound with my mouth."

"A cow!"

"Good, Bobbie, you guessed it. Now who am I? I have two legs. I do my work by walking and sometimes riding in a car. I carry a large pack on my shoulder. I visit many houses each day."

I thought I knew that one. "Is it a paperboy?"

"Nice try, Son, but that's not what I have in mind. When driving the car, this person sometimes drives on the wrong side of the street."

I was about to say a mailman, but Megan said it first.

"Yes, that's it. Good guess, Megan."

"Who am I?" Mom asked us again. "I live in your yard. I am green."

"Grass?"

"No, but keep guessing, Bobbie. I have a trunk and long arms. I turn colors in the fall."

"A tree!" Bobbie shouted. She shouts the answer a lot because she gets so excited.

"Right, Bobbie. Now who am I? I have four legs. People use me when they eat. I am in your dining room."

"Is it a chair?" Megan asked.

Mom looked in the rearview mirror so she could see us in the backseat. "No, but you're very close. People put food and plates on me while they eat."

Then I knew the answer. "A table!"

"Right, Toph." Then Mom thought for a second. "Who am I? I have two legs. I like to walk. The Bible talks about me, especially in the New Testament. I am a good man. I love everybody, including children. I teach people about God."

Megan guessed that it was Moses.

"No, but you're right that He's someone from the Bible." Mom gave us some more clues. "I was born in a barn. I never had a house to live in. I had twelve special friends who followed Me around trying to learn all about Me."

I tried to answer. "Paul?"

"No, that's a good guess, Topher, but it's not right. This person loved to tell about Heaven. He did miracles."

"Jesus!" Bobbie shouted again. I pretended to plug my ears.

"Bobbie, you're right!" Mom smiled at Bobbie. Bobbie smiled a big smile too. I think she was proud for guessing the right answer.

"Mom, what was Jesus like?" she asked.

"Well, He came to earth as a baby to Joseph and Mary. He grew up like you, but He didn't sin—not even when He was a child. He probably worked with Joseph in the carpenter shop, making things from wood. When He became a man and started the work that His Heavenly Father gave Him, He began doing miracles and talking to crowds of people about God and Heaven."

"Did He talk to children?"

"Oh, yes. He liked children very much. The Bible tells us that Jesus let a child sit on His lap. He told the disciples to let the children come to Him. Parents wanted Jesus to bless their children."[1]

"What's 'bless'?"

"It's when Jesus put His hand on the children's heads and said kind words to them. Jesus would ask God to watch over the children and make them happy. To bless someone is to give kindness, praise, or goodness to him."

"I want to visit Jesus someday."

"If you believe He died for you, you will, Bobbie."

Verse to Read

Luke 2:52: "And Jesus increased in wisdom and stature, and in favour with God and man."

1. Matthew 19:13, 14; Mark 10:13, 14; Luke 18:15, 16

QUESTIONS TO ASK YOUR CHILD
✳

1. How was Jesus different from you when He was growing up?

2. How do you know Jesus loved children when He was grown up?

How Old
Is Jesus?

One Saturday Bobbie asked Mom if her friend Christy could come over to play. Mom said she could.

"Christy didn't used to live here. She used to live near a big lake in New York in the mountains. She said she was three when she lived there. Now she's four. Do people change ages when they move to a new place?" Bobbie asked.

"Only if it's their birthday. Moving doesn't change their

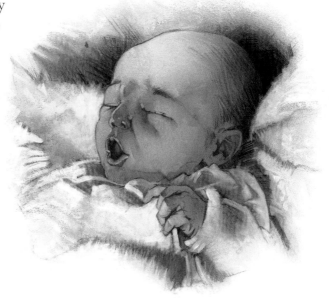

age. Christy had a birthday when she first came here; that's when her age changed."

"Oh." Bobbie looked like she was thinking about that. She went out the door, but then she came right back in again. "Mom, last night we looked at the picture of Mary and Joseph and baby Jesus in my Bible, remember? How old is Jesus now, Mom?"

"Bobbie, Jesus is God's Son. Jesus lives in Heaven with God forever and ever. He helped God make the world. Then He moved to earth and was a baby. We use the word 'eternal' to describe Him."

"What's 'eternal'?"

"Well, it means 'no beginning or ending.'"

"So Jesus is so old you couldn't count it?"

"Yes, that's right."

"Then how come He was a baby when He moved to earth? How come He didn't stay forever old?"

"When Jesus came to earth to live, He chose to come as a baby who grew up to be a man."

"How old was Jesus in earth years?"

"He got to be 33 years old, and then He died."

"How old is Daddy?"

"He's 33."

"Is he going to die?" Bobbie looked really scared for a second.

"No, honey. Daddy's healthy."

"But why did Jesus die when He was 33?"

"Because He had finished the job He had come to do. He went back to Heaven."

Verse to Memorize

Hebrews 1:8: "But unto the Son he saith, Thy throne, O God, is for ever and ever."

QUESTIONS TO ASK YOUR CHILD

✳

1. What does "eternal" mean?

2. How long did Jesus live on earth?

3. Who is eternal?

Where Does Jesus Live?

I have a giant roadway cloth that I lay on the floor, and I drive my trucks and minicars on it. I usually play with it right after supper. Bobbie always wants to play too. I usually let her because it's no fun to play alone. When she plays with me, we pretend that we're going to someone's house and then to someone else's.

Sometimes we say we go to the governor's house. We use special voices. I pretend to knock on the door and ask, "Is this the governor's house?"

Bobbie pretends to be the maid. She likes to say, "By george, the governor does live here."

Then we can go to Uncle Pete's house. We take the long highway and pretend to go to Grandma and Grandpa's. I always want to go to Tommy's house, and Bobbie wants to go to Carrie's house and Melissa's house. We even go to visit famous baseball players like Babe Ruth and Hank Aaron. Of course I know it's all pretend, but I think Bobbie thinks it's real.

Last time I let Bobbie play with me even though I didn't really

want to. I was happy when
Mom told Bobbie it was time to
take a bath and get ready for bed.

"But I can't, Mom. I'm at the governor's house with Toph having
tea."

"You can, and you will by the time I count to three."

"Yes, Mom." Then Bobbie looked at me. "Governor, I must go home
now." Bobbie got up. She tried to take her time, but it didn't work. Mom
just put her hand on Bobbie's back and gently helped her. Bobbie started
walking toward the hallway.

"Mom, did Jesus ever live in Grafton?"

"No, Bobbie, He didn't."

"Did He ever live in Pennsylvania?" I could hear Bobbie asking
questions even when she started going up the stairs.

"No, Bobbie. When Jesus came to earth, He lived with His parents
in the town of Nazareth in a country called Israel. It's very far from
here, but it's a real place—just like Grafton where you live with Dad
and me."

49

I couldn't find my purple motorcycle, so I went upstairs to look for it in my room. I could still hear Bobbie asking questions.

"Where did Jesus live when He grew up?"

"Well, for most of that time He traveled around, telling people about God. The Bible says He never had a pillow or a place to call His home."[1]

"But where did He sleep and take a bath?"

"Well, Jesus had many friends such as Mary, Martha, and Lazarus. Sometimes He stayed with friends, and sometimes He slept outside on the ground under the stars."

"All by Himself?"

"He may have been alone sometimes, but He also had twelve men and sometimes many more who were with Him. He wasn't alone very often."

I found my motorcycle under my bed. I find lots of stuff under there. I took it into Bobbie's room. I kind of wanted to hear what Bobbie was asking.

"Hi, Toph. Mom, after Jesus died and came alive again, where did He live? In that big rock with the angel?"

"No, that was a grave for dead people. Jesus was alive again. He stayed on earth for forty days, then He left earth."

"Where'd He go? Did He go to the moon or out in space?"

"No, Bobbie, the Bible says Jesus went to be with God in Heaven."[2] I drove my motorcycle on Bobbie's bed and around her dolls' legs.

Bobbie kept talking. "What's Jesus doing in Heaven?"

"Oh, He talks to God about you and me."[3]

"Does He tell God when I'm bad?"

"No, actually He tells God how much He loves you. He's doing something else very important in Heaven."

"What?"

"He's making a place for all those who trust Him and love Him. They will go and live with Him forever."[4]

"Jesus has a place to live in, and all the people who love Him and trust Him get to go there too. I'd like to go to His house. I'll bet it's pretty."

"It is, Bobbie, because God the Father and Jesus are there."

Verse to Memorize

Hebrews 12:2: "Looking unto Jesus the author and finisher of our faith; who . . . endured the cross, despising the shame, and is set down at the right hand of the throne of God."

1. Matthew 8:20
2. Acts 1:11
3. 1 Timothy 2:5; Hebrews 7:25
4. John 14:3

QUESTIONS TO ASK YOUR CHILD

✳

1. Where is Jesus today?

2. What does Jesus do in Heaven?

3. How can you go to Heaven?

Can I Talk with Jesus?

Every time the phone rings, Bobbie wants to answer it. "I'll get it, Mom! Hello, this is the Schmidt house. How may I help you?" Mom and Dad taught Bobbie how to say that, but she doesn't always answer the phone the right way.

One time Mom was expecting a phone call from Dad. He was working someplace away from home. Mom told us, "If the phone rings this afternoon, don't answer it. I'll get it, you understand?"

Megan and I nodded, and Bobbie said, "Yes, Mom."

Tommy came over that day, and we played catch in the backyard. Megan and her friend Ginny were skipping rope. Bobbie kept bugging us. First she wanted to play with Megan and Ginny, but she kept messing up. It was pretty funny. Then she wanted to play with Tommy and me. She did for a while, but she must have been bored, because she went inside.

Bobbie got her shovel and pail to play in the sandbox. She was coming back outside when the phone rang. She ran to get it. I think she thought it was Dad.

"Hello, this is the Schmidt house. How may I help you?" She got it right that time.

But a scary voice said, "I have a collect—" Bobbie didn't even listen to what the man said. She dropped the phone on the floor and ran outside.

After Tommy and Ginny went home, Megan, Bobbie, and I went inside. We decided to play Trouble in the family room. I guess Mom walked by the phone and heard a loud buzzing—you know, that sound the phone makes when it's off the hook. So she came and found us.

"Did any of you children pick up the phone today?"

Bobbie asked, "Why?"

"I just found it off the hook. I wondered why Dad didn't call. That's not like him. He said he would call this afternoon."

Megan and I looked at Bobbie. "Umm, uhh, umm. I picked up the phone when I came in to get a toy. I said 'How may I help you?' like I'm supposed to, but this very scary voice said something so I just dropped the phone and ran."

"Dropped it and ran? Bobbie, didn't you talk with the person on the phone?"

"No, he was scary! He said something 'bout collect, and I didn't know what to do. I went outside and forgot to tell you."

I could tell Mom wasn't too happy. "Bobbie Lynn, if you can't answer the phone politely, you may not answer it at all. Besides, you disobeyed. I asked you children not to answer the phone today."

"But I wanted to talk to Daddy. I thought it was him. When I heard that other man, I didn't know what to do."

"That's why I asked you not to answer the phone. Dad planned to call collect, and whoever answered the phone needed to accept the charges. That was Dad calling."

"It wasn't Daddy's voice."

"No, you heard the operator who was trying to help Dad make his call. Since you dropped the phone, Dad wasn't able to get through. He must be wondering if we're okay."

Dad called again that night, but Mom wouldn't let Bobbie talk with him. It was a punishment, and Bobbie cried. "But I love Daddy, and I wanna talk to him."

"Bobbie, I know you love Dad, and he loves you. He told me to tell you that."

"But I wanted to talk to him myself. I miss him." She kept sniffling.

"Dad is working at a special project where he doesn't have a phone. He has to make a trip to town to call us. You may talk with him tomorrow when he calls."

"But I want to talk with him now." I wondered if Bobbie would ever stop crying.

"Next time you should listen better and obey."

Finally Bobbie did stop crying and wiped her nose with her hand. Yuck! Mom didn't like it either, so she gave Bobbie a tissue.

"Mom, does Jesus have a phone in Heaven? Would He ever call collect? That man sounded like Jesus."

I kind of rolled my eyes 'cause I knew Jesus wouldn't have a scary voice. Bobbie was trying to dis-, dis-, dis—I know the word. I've heard Mom say it—distrack or something like that. Bobbie was trying to "distrack" Mom.

"No, dear. Jesus doesn't need a phone."

"Why?"

"Because He and His Father talk with you through the Bible."

"Can I talk to Him?"

"Yes, by praying to Him."

"But I can't hear His voice."

"Yes, but you can talk with Him anytime, even if you don't have a phone. You can talk to God when you're in trouble or when you're happy or when you're alone or when you're with many people. And you don't have to bother with an operator either. You can talk to God the Father through Jesus at any time."

"That's better than a phone. Can I talk to God right now?"

"What will you tell Him?"

"I think I'll tell Him I'm sorry for disobeying you."

"He would like to hear that."

Verse to Memorize

John 15:16: "That whatsoever ye shall ask of the Father in my name, he may give it you."

QUESTIONS TO ASK YOUR CHILD

1. *How does Jesus talk to you?*

2. *How can you talk to God?*

3. *When should you talk to God?*

Does Jesus Have Brothers or Sisters?

Last month at school Megan studied about families. One night we were cleaning off the table after supper when she told Mom she needed help drawing a family tree. It was going to go on the bulletin board at school.

Sometimes Bobbie sits at the table and colors while Megan and I do our homework. I think it makes her feel like a big girl. That night she got off her chair and stood next to Megan. "You're drawing Mom, Dad, Toph, and me up in a tree? That's silly."

"No, Bobbie." Megan started talking like a mom again. "I'm drawing a picture of all the people in our family and all the other people in Mom's and Dad's families too. A family tree is a way to show who is related to whom." Megan says there is a difference between "who" and "whom," and when she uses those words she thinks she sounds really grown-up.

I guess Bobbie didn't understand about the tree because she shook her head. "Toph and you and me are in Mom and Dad's family. That's all there is. We don't have anyone else."

"Oh, Bobbie. You know Dad was in a family before Toph and you and I were born. Mom grew up in a family too. They each had brothers and sisters and their own mom and dad."

"Oh yeah. But why are you drawing them in a tree?"

"I'm not. It's just a way to put it on paper so we can see who is related to whom." There she went again with that "whom" stuff.

Then she asked Mom, "How many brothers and sisters do you have?"

"Two brothers and one sister."

"How many brothers and sisters does Dad have?"

"He has one brother and two sisters."

"Their children are my cousins, right?"

Mom just nodded. Bobbie asked a question. "How about me? Who are my cousins? I want to be up in the family tree too." She was watching Megan draw the tree.

"Mom, does Jesus have a family tree?"

"You mean did Jesus have any brothers and sisters? Well, yes, when He lived here on earth."

"Did He have anyone like Megan and Toph?" I couldn't imagine Jesus having a little sister like Bobbie.

But Mom said, "The Bible tells us Jesus actually had several brothers. One was named James, and there were others. The Bible mentions that Jesus had sisters too."[1]

Bobbie said she knew Jesus' mom's name. "It was Mary."

"You're right. Many people think Joseph was Jesus' father. But actually God was Jesus' father, and Joseph got to take care of Jesus while He lived here on earth. We sometimes call Joseph Jesus' earthly father."

"Did Jesus have anyone else?"

"Yes, Bobbie. The Bible says that anyone who would do the will of God in Heaven could be related to Jesus and be His mother and sister and brother."

"Wow! He must need the biggest tree for His family! Are you in God's family tree?"

"Yes, I am, and Grandpa and Grandma Williams are too."

"How come I'm not in God's family tree?"

"Because so far you haven't asked Jesus to be your Savior."

Verses to Read

Matthew 12:47, 48, 50: "Then one said unto him, Behold, thy mother and thy brethren stand [outside], desiring to speak with thee. But he answered and said unto him that told him, Who is my mother? And who are my brethren? . . . For whosoever shall do the will of my Father which is in heaven, the same is my brother, and sister, and mother."

1. Matthew 13:55, 56

QUESTIONS TO ASK YOUR CHILD

✳

1. Did Jesus have brothers and sisters on earth?

2. Does Jesus have brothers and sisters in Heaven?

3. How can you become a part of God's family?

Why Did Jesus Die?

We have a great dog named Shep. He plays in the yard with me. We go fishing too, and he helps me pick up sticks. He's one of my best friends. I think Shep is the bravest dog in the whole town. He barks at noises in the night and keeps us safe. Shep sleeps by my bed because he's mostly my dog.

One day last summer, Megan came running home. Mom and I were in the kitchen doing something. I don't remember what. Megan was out of breath because she had run as fast as she could. She kept gulping for air. "There's . . . a fire . . . on the Boyces' . . . old barn . . . I saw . . . Shep down there . . . Hurry up!"

"A fire at the Boyces' barn? What's Shep doing down there?" Mom was already going out the door. Of course I went too. I had to find Shep.

Megan told us, "He's barking by the back barn door. He won't come when I call him. I'm afraid he's going to go inside."

Mom called Bobbie, and we ran the whole way to the Boyces'. When we got there, I didn't see Shep anywhere. I yelled for him over and over. The fire trucks were there, and lots of people started coming to watch. I walked all the way around the barn. I had to stay pretty far away from it since the fire was very hot. I couldn't get close enough to see inside.

Then I heard Shep barking. It sounded quiet, as if he was far away. But I knew it was Shep, and I followed the sound. It wasn't coming from the barn; it was coming from the field. I found Shep lying on the ground with three tiny kittens. He was licking them and trying to clean them up. Shep seemed really tired or something.

He tried to get up when he saw me, but he couldn't. I knew the kittens were the Boyces'. They had just been born last week. I knew 'cause Ginny showed them to Megan and me. The sad thing was that the kittens' mother had been hit by a car and killed. The Boyces fed the kittens with an eyedropper. Shep must have known they were in the barn and gone to rescue them! "Good dog, Shep! Good dog!" I patted him on the head and petted the kittens too.

Then I remembered that Mom would be worried. Whenever I forget that, I get in trouble. So I ran back to tell Mom that I had found Shep. Mom, Megan, Bobbie, and I stayed until the firemen finished putting out the fire. The back of the barn was pretty messed up, but Mom said a fireman told Mr. Boyce that he could probably build that part again.

I went back to Shep in the field. Mom brought him some water. I was getting a little afraid because he seemed hurt. He tried to get up but couldn't. "Mom, what's wrong with Shep? Why can't he walk?"

"He may have gotten too close to the flames and smoke. It may have hurt his lungs."

"He'll be okay, won't he?"

"We'll have to wait and see."

Mom went home, but she had Megan bring me my wagon. Megan helped me put Shep into the wagon; then I pulled him home. Mom lifted him out of the wagon and laid him on a huge towel on the back porch.

Bobbie seemed worried too. "Why did Shep get hurt, Mom? Why did he save those kittens?"

"He's a brave dog, Bobbie. He didn't even think about himself; he only wanted to help the kittens."

"But Shep almost died."

"Yes, he is very weak, Bobbie. He was willing to get hurt to save the kittens. They have no mother, and they were too weak to help themselves. Shep is a brave dog."

"Jesus was very brave when He died, right?"

"Yes, braver than Shep because He knew ahead of time the cruel things that were going to happen to Him, and He was so strong that He could have stopped those soldiers. He could have called for ten thousand angels to rescue Him, but He didn't."

Bobbie didn't really get it. "Why would Jesus let the soldiers kill Him, Mom? Did He do something bad?"

"No, nothing. Jesus was perfect. He never did anything wrong. Some men lied about Jesus at His trial."

"Is that the picture in Bobbie's Bible?" I asked that. I remembered seeing it the first day Bobbie got the Bible.

"Yes, it is." Mom smiled at me, but then she looked at Bobbie and Megan. "Jesus died to rescue you."

Bobbie made a goofy face. "But I'm not in a fire!"

"Not now, but if you don't trust Jesus as your Savior by accepting His death for you on the cross, you will face punishment in a place called Hell."

"I don't want to be punished."

"Jesus died so that you wouldn't have to be punished." Mom looked at Bobbie, then Megan, and then me. "If any of you would like to tell God you are a sinner and need Him to save you, I want you to feel free to talk to me." Mom smiled and told us again, "Jesus will save you, if you ask Him to."

Verses to Memorize

1 Corinthians 15:3, 4: "Christ died for our sins according to the scriptures; And that he was buried, and that he rose again the third day according to the scriptures."

John 3:16: "For God so loved the world that He gave His only begotten Son, that whoever believes in Him should not perish but have everlasting life" (NKJV).

QUESTIONS TO ASK YOUR CHILD

*

1. *Why did Jesus die?*

2. *What happens if you don't ask Jesus to be your Savior?*

3. *Have you asked Jesus to be your Savior?*

Is Jesus Alive Now?

During the summer, our town has Summerfest. It's fun! We play games and ride on this small train. You have to pay to ride a horse or a tractor. People set up booths to sell stuff. Mom calls it "old junk." I guess some of it looks like junk, but some of it is cool. A band plays music most of the time, and all the people walk around, buy junk, and eat food. I try to save my allowance for a long time so I have money to spend at Summerfest.

The people from the animal shelter have a booth too. My favorite part of Summerfest is the animals. Last year they had a cute little black dog with white spots. They had a cocker spaniel with really soft long ears too. They had kittens, but I didn't like them as much as the puppies. And there were tiny rabbits.

I asked my dad probably ten times if I could have a puppy, but he always said, "No, you don't take care of Shep that well. Our family doesn't need another animal for your mother to clean up after."

"But I will take care of it." I told him that, and I meant it! I even promised.

Dad finally said maybe I could get some goldfish. That way, he told me, I could prove myself with a smaller animal. So on our way home from Summerfest, we went to the pet store and bought six goldfish: two for me, two for Bobbie, and two for Megan. We bought some fish food and a little fishbowl too.

We named our fish in the car. Mine were Tiger and Spotty. Megan called hers Splish and Splash. Bobbie named hers Whitey and Goldie.

We remembered to feed our fish every day, but after some days, Goldie started looking kind of tired or something. He just hung around the top of the bowl and didn't swim very much. Dad said he was sick. The next day he was floating at the top of the water. Mom had to tell Bobbie that Goldie was dead. Bobbie wasn't sure. "Maybe he'll come back alive again."

"Bobbie, I know it's sad, but Goldie is not alive. He got sick and died. He's not going to get better. We need to get rid of him before he starts smelling up the room."

"We need to wait two more days, Mom. Please!" Bobbie was going to start crying any second. I could tell.

Mom told her the fish would not come back to life. It would not work to wait.

"Yes, it will. I know it."

After two days, we couldn't see inside the fishbowl anymore because the water was so cloudy. I plugged my nose when I got close to it. It stank! And Goldie was still dead. Then Bobbie cried and cried and she kept saying, "It worked in the Bible. It worked in the Bible."

I tried to figure out what she was talking about. "What do you mean, Bobbie, 'It worked in the Bible'? Mom didn't read about any goldfish in the Bible."

"When Jesus died, He came alive again after three days."

Mom hugged Bobbie and tried to explain things. "Bobbie, God brought Jesus back to life. It was a miracle. A miracle is a great and mighty work that only God can do. God brought Jesus back to life to prove that Jesus is His Son and that He had forgiven our sins. God wanted us to know that Jesus is also God. Jesus is the only One Who ever came back to life by Himself after He died."

"Oh." Bobbie wasn't crying anymore—at least not as hard. "Maybe God will do it again?"

"Well, Bobbie, Jesus did such a special work that the same event doesn't need to happen again. Because it happened only once, it makes Jesus' coming back alive that much more important. The Bible says that Jesus will come for us and take us to be with Him forever."[1]

Verse to Memorize

Matthew 28:6: "He is not here: for he is risen, as he said. Come, see the place where the Lord lay."

1. John 14:3

QUESTIONS TO ASK YOUR CHILD
✳

1. What is a miracle?

2. Why did God raise Jesus from the dead?

3. Is Jesus alive today?

Farewell to Adult Readers

We hope you have been strengthened as you, your child, grandchild, or a neighbor child have learned more about the God of the universe and the God of you and me. He wants to be your God. If you have not already settled that matter you need to do so soon. As my coauthor Robert Newman can now attest: life is short; judgment without Christ is sure; and eternity is real. Make sure you and your loved ones have your reservations for Heaven cared for.

Romans 10:13 assures all of us that "whosoever shall call upon the name of the Lord shall be saved." I called out to him as a six-year-old ready to begin first grade. He has been my God from that day till now. He has made my life worth living.

Admit your need of a Savior; call out to Him like a child does for help; and accept His free gift. While none of us will ever be good enough to deserve Heaven, none of us has done anything so bad that we can't be forgiven.